A Degree in Homelessness?
Entrepreneurial Skills for Students

Glen Dunzweiler

Copyright © 2019 by Glen Dunzweiler

All rights reserved, including the right to reproduce this book, or portions thereof, in any form. No part of this book may be used or reproduced in any manner whatsoever without written permission from the author, except in the case of brief quotations embodied in critical articles and reviews. The views expressed herein are the responsibility of the author and do not necessarily represent the position of the publisher. For information or permission, write: [glen@glendunzweiler.com].

This is a work of creative nonfiction. The events herein are portrayed to the best of the author's memory. While all the stories in this book are true, some names and identifying details may have been changed to protect the privacy of the people involved.

Editorial work by Scott Fields and Eschler Editing
Cover design by Rob Dario
Photograph of Glen Dunzweiler by JoséAngel Donado Interior print design and layout by Glen Dunzweiler. eBook design and layout by Glen Dunzweiler.

Published by Glen Dunzweiler

First Edition: November 2019
Printed in the United States of America

In loving memory of Orene Dunzweiler - a dedicated teacher.

Dedicated To
Jonah and Maia Chaffin

Acknowledgements
Thank you to:

Rob Dario for being my graphic collaborator all of these years.

Elena Perez for helping to get this book out there.

The following people inspired me to write this book:

Grant Baldwin

Drew Dalzell

Steve Harrison

Nancy Fulton

Rob Kosberg

Joe Nicassio

Andre Simoneau

Bo Siton

Supporters

The following people helped me to put this book into your hands:

<u>VIP</u>

Elizabeth Chatten

Phyllis Dunzweiler, Joy and Melissa Duncan

Shannon Eagles

Kris Errecart

Raul Perez

Jorge Salomone and Niccole Dunn

Tobie and Molly

<u>Platinum</u>

Laurie Braddy

Kris Dietrich

Shelly Farley Kirkland

Dorothy Tarr

TABLE OF CONTENTS

FOREWORD	08
PART ONE – DEPROGRAMMING	13
WHAT WE DON'T TEACH	14
WHY GO TO COLLEGE?	18
THE POWER OF EDUCATION	22
THE STRATEGIC EDUCATION	24
THE POWER OF WORK EXPERIENCE	30
THE POWER OF A GROUP	32
THE POWER OF TEACHING	35
FIND YOUR STRENGTH	37
DEFINING YOUR BRAND	41
PART TWO – THE BUSINESS PART	43
BUSINESS IS NOT THE DEVIL	44
THE MYTH OF THE SLEAZY SALESMAN	46
THE BUSINESS MINDSET	48
PAY YOURSELF	51
THE COST OF VALUE	53
THE SLIDING VALUE OF TIME	56
THE SLIDING REALITY OF MONEY	58
FREEING MONEY FROM MORALITY	61
FINDING OPPORTUNITIES	64
BUILDING INTEREST	67
UNDERSTANDING MOTIVATIONS	71
YOU HAVE TO SELL	74
BEING SCALABLE	76
AUTOMATION	78
FOCUS VERSUS DIVERSIFICATION	80
THE TIME IT TAKES TO BUILD A BUSINESS	82
ENTREPRENEURIAL CONFIDENCE	85
FINDING THE THING YOU ENJOY DOING FOR PEOPLE	87
REINVENTING THE WHEEL	89
CONCLUSION	91

FOREWORD

Hello, students! Welcome to a book that challenges most everything you've ever been taught about how to succeed in this world.

When it came to education, I was told to follow my passion, and I always did. But I never put a value on how much money my passion would make me. I was taught that to think about money was to cheapen your endeavors. I was told to do it for the love of doing it!

The fact is, we live in a capitalist society, and no one's going to pay you to follow your passion. "Follow your passion" is an inspiration not backed by reality. Those who simply follow their passion turn their passion into success by applying business skills, finding a business partner, and/or building (having) a fan base willing to support them. The other side of this is that there are businesspeople who make money off people who follow their passion. As a passionate person, your job is to not get suckered.

Do you want to
- Make money?
- Take your life into your own hands?
- Solve the income/expense/success puzzle?
- Succeed at life outside of school?

This book is an entrepreneurial business primer for the unprimed. I have spent a lot of my life succeeding but hitting huge barriers I did not understand how to get past. But I have spent the last four years exploring those barriers—what they are and how to overcome them. And that's what's in these pages—my insights, illustrated by the experiences of successful businesspeople I have met.

Though I will talk about a new way to look at education, let me be clear: In NO way is this book an argument for you to stay away from college. In EVERY way, it challenges you to think about how you will use the education you receive.

I'm pretty much an academic from front to back. I grew up in a household with two teachers as parents and then spent eleven years teaching at universities. I was taught that if you wanted more money, you went to school and got a piece of paper that certified you had more knowledge. Then you could apply for jobs that required that certificate—and they were supposed to pay more money. One problem, though. My education and degree didn't mean I knew how to make money. I only knew how to get a job. When I found myself stuck and unable to convince employers that I was worth more money, I realized I was doing something wrong.

What if you don't care about making money?
and
Why should you read this book?

Simply put, everyone cares about money, even those who say they don't. But people care about it in different ways. Some folks care about having enough to buy a hamburger, while others care about having enough to purchase a Tesla. I have been where I did not have enough to buy a hamburger. It's no fun. So if you like eating, you should read this book.

In 2015, I quit my teaching position and moved to Los Angeles to focus on business. Though I struggled to buy a burger, I put the time to good use. I began learning how other people made money, how I could make money, what it takes to create something of value for people, and how to get that product to a market that perceives its value.

Meanwhile, I kept in touch with my students. I could feel their concern about huge student-loan debt and their uncertainty about how they could use their degree to secure work after graduation. As I came to understand what people really value and how to help folks attain it, I began to let these students in on a few strategies for monetary success post–formal education.

Unless you have parents who can teach you business concepts, you do not learn business as part of your core education. Oddly enough, the economy we live in works on the back of business, and so this puts a huge part of the population at a disadvantage.

I want to keep students and ex-students out of poverty and insurmountable debt. That's my motivation for writing this book.

It's important for those who are not business-minded to understand certain business concepts. With that in mind, this is a business book for the layperson—the person who has been told to follow their dream and their passion but has not been instructed how to fuse those dreams with making money; the person who is told to go to college or to get a job because that is simply what we do; the person who does not have a clear and defined exit strategy for life after school. The goal here is to give these students a fighting chance.

Ready to Fight?

Your fighting chance begins in the first part of this book, where we'll discuss education as it stands and the strategy I've found for success. In my talks, I call it "Learn, Do, Connect, Repeat." Some of my shortcomings and failures are documented so that you may learn from them as well.

In the second part of the book, we'll cover business and entrepreneurial concepts I feel are important for everyone to know— whether you're a current or recently graduated student, or you can barely remember when you were a student. I have spent a lot of time and money uncovering some universal business truths, and the things I share not only come from successful people but from successful people with integrity.

Feel free to share your thoughts after reading this book. I look forward to hearing your questions, insights, and critiques. You can reach me at my website: glendunzweiler.com.

And now, let's dive in.

PART ONE—DEPROGRAMMING

WHAT WE DON'T TEACH

We Don't Teach Business.

In academia, unless a student is taking business classes, they rarely learn about the business concepts and mechanisms that drive their field of study. A few programs have begun to address this, but for most departments, preparing students for the world outside academia is not the focus.

What's more, sometimes the business backing the field of study is solely the business of teaching itself. It's academia for academia's sake. Academia is often seen as a necessary sanctuary of study away from the "real world," but this view is throwing graduates out into poverty—in a world they are totally unequipped to survive, much less thrive, in.

Let me say that another way: we love selling the *idea* of education without preparing our students for the *reality* after education. Case in point: My graduate school insisted I have no outside work while I was in the program (in part because there was no extra time in the program for outside work). That left me with only the summers to set up work relationships outside the academic realm. The result? Upon finishing graduate school, I was the proverbial baby bird jumping out of the tree.

Universities face the conundrum all businesses face when marketing themselves. You focus on the positive and don't point out the negative. If you tell a student what he or she needs to hear (we will be teaching you esoteric knowledge in a field that likely won't prepare you to earn a living or function after you graduate), they are not likely to enter your institution. Instead, institutions tell potential students how fun, amazing, competitive, and cool your degree program is. They confirm to their "customer" that they are making the right choice. Very few programs can put their realities out front and still have applicants to accept.

How Do We Address This Fundamental Problem?

- **Creating a personal business plan from day one in college**
    - I think departments have a conflict of interest here, and maybe campus career centers need to be expanded so they connect with every student who is accepted while subsequently developing a personal business plan with that student. This plan would need to be adapted and adhered to every year. For an eighteen- to twenty-two-year-old, this isn't the fun stuff, but it's the stuff that can keep them off the streets or out of their parents' basements.
    - Instead of marketing themselves with "Come here because . . . ," a university could promote their programs with "If you come here, this is how you will succeed once you leave."
- **In-class reinforcement**
    - However, I don't think the burden of a student's success after academia falls solely on the career

center. Every student needs to be encouraged to think of their choices within an economic construct. If instructors would do this through class reminders and examples, students would be better prepared to be monetarily stable members of society postgraduation. As educators, we know that people hear the same thing in different ways. And as marketers, we know we need our audience to become familiar with our ideas or products before they can adopt them. Money management and economic realization constitute a life view, and, like health, people need to be able to knowledgeably view every choice through that lens.

- I propose that small economic conversations be held in every class—if only to spark interest. This may sound like beating a subject over a student's head, but we never know when a message will ring true. Just as we are always conscious of our personal physical and mental health, we should always be aware of our personal economic health. I don't know that instructors are necessarily prepared for this line of thought, but it never hurts for a student to start asking questions. Just remember to formulate the best question you can and to be sensitive when asking it. Hijacking lectures to ask, "When are we ever going to use this knowledge?" is never a good strategy.

What It Looks Like
When we teach anything, we
- *Demonstrate*
- *Convey*

- *Challenge*
- *Support*
- *Correct*
- *Repeat*

When we learn, we
- *Absorb*
- *Think*
- *Process/relate*
- *Strategize*
- *Do*

If I had to break down the process for all teaching and learning, that would be it. The same goes for teaching and learning business concepts within the context of your specific field of study. Business underpins every other field of study. Without business to generate capital and flow it through the system, other nonrevenue-generating ventures couldn't happen. For example, an archaeologist might not be able to perform their work without the large grants and endowments bestowed to their institution.

In my estimation, we should be teaching business like we teach reading, mathematics, and science.

WHY GO TO COLLEGE?

This is a question you should always be asking yourself. The answer must be personal and motivated by strategic thinking. Here are a few possible responses:

1. Knowledge
2. Prestige and visibility
3. A degree
4. A network of people
5. An escape from people
6. Procrastination on a life decision
7. An escape from world pressures

No matter your motivation for attending college, you must look at it as a tool you can use to build your future. If you're not going to use this tool, is it really for you? Knowledge is arguably the most valuable of the specific tools you will gain from a university, but the structured knowledge you get in a class setting may not be the most pertinent information you gain from your college experience.

For example, understanding how to get your campus meal plan worked out can teach you about the intricacies of policies and bureaucracies and even about the buffers people establish so they don't have to be held accountable for offering you the food you aren't allergic to or the special dietary needs that you requested.

Ann's College Experience

My friend Ann learned a lot about adulthood by leaving her family and attending a four-year university. She learned about parking tickets, landlords, boyfriends, laundromats, and the art of negotiation (convincing an early-childhood-development instructor to pass her based on her pregnancy).

Interestingly, she does not remember much about her classwork. She studied psychology and found her major to be interesting but not her focus. She didn't start really paying attention to her academic pursuits until after graduation when she found that working on loan documents for a bank was unsatisfying and that she would much rather teach elementary school.

Thankfully, her degree in psychology wasn't useless. Putting her alma mater on her résumé meant something to some employers and helped her get hired. The name brand of her university helped build her personal brand. In fact, some employers will actually headhunt at a particular school because of that school's reputation. Ann wasn't recruited, but her school was part of a system that was, and still is, well-known.

Her degree also became a stepping-stone because it was required for entry into a credentialing program for teachers.

Ann does not regret her undergraduate choice because it enabled her to escape small-town life and experience college in a destination city. And even though she is still heavily in debt because of it, she looks back on those years fondly. To her, it was a five-year working vacation.

Still, could she have enjoyed a more satisfying and financially rewarding outcome had she approached college as a business tool from the beginning?

Don't Use College to Buy Time

Jim was making a living as a copywriter but saw his industry shrinking and opted to go back to school to preempt job termination. In a perfect world, he would have found a program that gave him the knowledge and training he needed to be back in demand. However, this is not what happened. Though armed with a new degree, Jim found himself in a job market just as depressed as the copywriting market. He ended up selling pool supplies, and if that wasn't unfortunate enough, the pool supply store closed. Jim had to sell everything and move in with a friend in order to avoid being homeless.

While Jim thought he was going to college to get training for a career jump, he was instead buying time to figure out what he wanted to do. In general, I have not heard of happy endings for those who "run away" to college to reset their career path. I'm sure those happy endings exist, but I don't see this strategy as a smart choice. It certainly isn't proactive.

You don't have to be midcareer like Jim to attend college to buy time. If you're thinking about going to college at any age, you should reflect on whether you're running to a tool that will set you up for a prosperous, rewarding life—or if you're running from not quite knowing what you want to do.

When you run *from* something instead of *to* something, you set yourself up for failure. If you want to succeed, you have to think ahead, not just react. You should absolutely get away from the bad things in life, but you should also develop a plan—otherwise you put yourself at risk for getting lost.

People admire and criticize college at the same time. It is recognized as some sort of marker for success, but then it is attacked for its methodology, cost, course offerings, faculty, or myriad other things.

Try to get to the bottom of *why* you're going, recognize that your education is simply a tool, and then develop a plan for how you want to use that tool.

THE POWER OF EDUCATION

Why Do We Learn? Why Do We Teach?

As you consider your reasons for going or not going to college, it's fair to ask, why do we learn after high school? Simply put, we have found that the more folks know, the more stable and prosperous society becomes. Education gives us a worldview that is more than the reality right in front of us.

Below is a quick and general breakdown of degree types:

Associate's and Bachelor's Degrees
General education courses were developed to promote a breadth of knowledge that developed a student's ability to broadly problem-solve situations. Specific knowledge is taught in both degrees, but the focus is on a broad education and not the achievement of a specific skill.

Trade Schools and Certificate Programs
Geared to develop specific vocational skills.

Master's Degrees
Geared to develop field-specific thoughts.

Doctorates and Specialized Degrees (MD, JD, MFA, BFA, etc.)
Focused on original research and professional practice.

Which Degree Is Right for You?

I was fortunate in my education because my parents were intelligent and insightful people who prospered as a result of their education, became educators, instilled in me the need for critical thinking, and encouraged me to grow while not dictating anything other than my need to succeed and to be a good person.

Not all people have that kind of background. Some parents are not so intelligent or educated and dictate their child's life direction based on different values.

No matter what your background is, it's challenging to decide what type of degree to work toward. I have been approached by multiple students seeking help in solving this conundrum. The following is a quick synopsis of how I try to match a student's proclivities with degree type to create a strategic, return-on-investment approach to education.

THE STRATEGIC EDUCATION

Realizing that any education you get is simply a tool and not the end product frees you to decide what you will do with that tool. You need to expect something from your education. You have to justify the investment of time and dollars. Education is valuable in and of itself, but you always need to look at the full investment and the proposed return.

Below are several things to consider as you think about how to use your education as a tool. You'll want to think about everything from the types of fields available, to market conditions, to following your passions.

Fields of Work and Study
- The Trades
    - My grandfather did not want to go to school. My great-grandfather told him that if he stopped going to school, he would teach him to be a bricklayer. Even though learning a trade on a jobsite is an informal education, it's still an education. You acquire information you don't already have. My grandfather laid brick for boilers and fireplaces until he got older. He then moved to a job with the city that (at the time) provided a stable income for his family. (This system of stable, well-paying trade is not necessarily a viable type of work anymore—depending on the trade.)

- Academics

- My father stayed in school and learned music from a teacher who changed his life. Because of this, he attained his credentials to teach music. He remained a music teacher until retirement but did, at one point, go after his master's degree to qualify for an administrative job, although that position was cut from his district, and he abandoned the program.

- The Arts
  - My dad used his education and aptitude for music to play in dance bands in junior high. He and his friends would get paid to play at dances and parties. In the 1950s and 1960s, sound systems were in their infancy, and prerecorded music was not used, other than in bars and on radio and TV. At the time, there was a market for what he could offer. But he shared with me that, in adulthood, he didn't want to be a gigging musician because he knew that lifestyle was not compatible with trying to raise a family.

- The STEM Fields
  - My neighbor started working for a large aerospace company right out of high school. He swept floors for them, but they liked him, saw potential, and paid for his engineering degree in exchange for six years of service to the company. He became an optical engineer but later wanted to work for himself so he could own his patents. STEM fields often maintain the employment funnels other industries have had to let go of.

Job Market Conditions

and Other Considerations

The instability of historic stability—Historically stable careers are no longer necessarily stable and can lock you into a pay scale that doesn't keep pace with our modern, volatile cost of living. Earning a fixed income for the long game is no longer a safe bet. It often shackles employees to a sinking ship, or worse, keeps them rowing, sedated and stupefied, in the ship's bowels until it throws them overboard into the shark-infested waters of capitalism.

In our modern economic landscape, if you are proactive in strategizing about the returns your education can give you, your education can provide you with a flotation device.

My friend Ann, the elementary school teacher, has seen her stability erode as the economic landscape has reacted to solve short-term demands rather than develop long-term strategies. For six years, she saw coworkers routinely "pink-slipped" at the end of the school year as a result of the 2008 economic crisis. The pink slip meant they had to wait until the beginning weeks of the next school year to see if they'd be offered a teaching contract again. She found herself one year of seniority away from a pink slip, and she saw a hiring freeze put a seven-year gap between herself and her newer colleagues. She was constantly waiting for the ax to drop and was fortunate when it didn't.

We continue to see teachers struggle with "the salary they are given." We see other professions no longer guaranteeing healthy salaries.

The new education—The good news here is that *you* get to live an empowered life where you actively pull knowledge from various sources and are able to take stock of your worth. You get to build your own value engine.

Think of your knowledge, skills, and the products you can make as possessions in your house. Think of being prepared to move every year. Everything you have and accrue will become consciously strategic as you know you will have to address it later. You become adept at understanding what you have and how it will apply to your future. Both formal and informal education are now easily accessible through digital platforms, and growth is more in your hands than ever before.

Working with your education—Leading your own future may not sound fun. A lot of folks just want to relax and settle in. I wanted this as well. I used to view employment as a solid rock I could moor to as a respite while floating down the river of life. Now the landscape is more of an ocean with boats and flotation devices you sometimes have to create yourself. Maybe there's an ocean liner out there, but there is no guarantee even that ship won't sink.

If employers could regain a belief in the importance of loyalty, protected harbors might be built. But right now, employers are the ones constantly moving and building flotation devices so they can choose who to pluck out of the water and for how long. If they started to have trouble filling positions because their employees could float to other ships, they might start being more loyal to their employees. Loyalty eventually has to go both ways, but the game is to not make yourself vulnerable.

Following Your Passions—Profitably

Supporting yourself with your education—The way to avoid being vulnerable is to become educated in what people value and to leverage that education into a product or service people are eager to pay for. You might be educated in bricklaying, teaching, music, engineering, or psychology (Ann's major), but you must use that education to create value for a population willing to pay you for your knowledge, work, or product.

What do you do when you don't know what education you want? —Be aware of what you don't know and develop a strategy to learn all you can. While you are planning and checking out your options, work on ways to accelerate your success. Talk to people. Collect ideas. Try new things. The only caveat here is to always be thinking about your return on investment. And be aware that there are businesspeople who make their money off people who follow their passion. As a passionate person, your job is to not get suckered.

Exploiting your education—A huge buzz phrase in business is "passive income." Businesses are continually looking for ways to make money on previous work.

Institutions of higher education are looking to do so as well. They look to make bank on their name. A university invests time and effort into building a desirable brand that can be sold to those willing to pay for it. For example, the University of California system has brand recognition through past accomplishments and past high-profile graduates. Ivy League schools also have prestigious brands.

Look at your education as a business decision.

When you decide on a school or an education, ask yourself why you are getting it and make sure you can justify the expense with a rationally predicted outcome. All businesses will take your money. They will really take your money if they don't have to do any work. And they will continue to raise their profit margins (their tuition) until the market refuses to pay it.

If you buy an opportunity to take classes at Yale, ask yourself what you expect out of it. You might expect

1. To be introduced to wealthy and powerful families so you too can play the rich game.
2. A stamp of credibility that gives you leverage over other job applicants from lesser-known schools.
3. A world-class education in your field that gives you the tools to blaze trails in your chosen industry.

The point is that you need to expect something from your education. You have to justify the expense. Education is valuable, but, as mentioned, you always need to look at the full investment and the proposed return.

THE POWER OF WORK EXPERIENCE

Why do we have to actually *do* things? Isn't there a button for that?

Work experience is key to your strategic approach to education—and beyond. Do it right and it will be a springboard for each stop in your career. You build a body of work, prove you have the attributes necessary for success, and network with people who can help you down the road. Work experience makes you real to people who don't know you. It shows them you want to work and that you know what you are doing.

When I was a lighting designer for live entertainment, I learned three things. First, I needed to build a portfolio with tangible proof of my skills. Second, working for well-known and well-regarded theatre companies let me piggyback off their reputation. In other words, if I was good enough to get hired by *x* company, I must be worth hiring. Third, the people I worked with at a company could then become references for me and attest to my competence and character.

Variety versus Stability—A Balance
The trick to valuable work experience is to find the balance between stability (demonstrating your dependability and consistency by working for one company) and variety (working with or for many companies).

Depending on your industry, the people you work with or for may value one over the other. I know that the longer I worked at my second university teaching job, the less attractive I became to supervisors for new jobs at that university. When I initially came to the university from out of town, I was exotic to the department chair and faculty. But the longer I stayed, the less exotic (and therefore the less valuable) I was perceived. Experience notwithstanding, there are companies that value hiring from within, and if you can find one, growing with them can be beneficial.

When I was a lifeguard just out of high school, one of the clubs I worked at became suspicious of the number of places I had previously worked. They suspected I was continuously getting "chased out of town." I had to convince them I just wanted to experience variety. Fortunately it worked. In such instances where a potential employer may question the number of jobs you've worked, letters of recommendation can help.

Invest in More Than Academics During Your College Years
The biggest thing work experience gives you is work experience. It's integral to success. Your network or degree or the prestige of an award may get you the job, but your work experience sets you up for success. Do as much as you can and then push to do more. When you get bored, do something to be able to expand your experiences. But *do* things. It can be your buffer against any doubt that may come from those around you regarding your work ethic and experience.

THE POWER OF A GROUP

Do I Really Have to Join a Group? Do I Have to Network?

Can't I just stay in my room and build my empire from there?

We cannot do everything on our own—something that took me awhile to learn. Few people can create success apart from others. This key insight will help you in college and in the real world. For those of us who are more comfortable lone-wolfing it, it can take a while to acquire this skill.

My independent streak started with my dad. He taught me that if I wanted something done right, I had to do it myself. He also taught me if I owned or worked with something, that within reason, I should know how to repair it; otherwise I had to make three times the money to have the same stuff.

Given the planned obsolescence of today's products, I don't know that his second lesson is so applicable anymore. But what these two lessons did do is make me very independent. When I was looking to be hired, sometimes my independence actually gave me an advantage because my autonomy and tenacity cost employers less money. For example, I didn't call IT when my computer had problems. I fixed it myself. This, however, led to a mentality among my superiors where they thought I needed less support, and they started piling on more work because "Glen can do it." Keeping my head down and working independently sometimes got me taken for granted.

When you run your own company, this overtly independent mentality can be a detriment because you tend to spend time burying yourself in a task rather than running your business and delegating. Learning to work with (and depend on) people is paramount.

Working with other people can actually enhance efficiency as long as each member is self-directed enough. Of course, managing a group dynamic is a fine balancing act; in large organizations, working with others can lead to bureaucracy, with jobs being divided for the sake of creating jobs.

So, How Do You Create a Group?

At some point, you may strike out on your own, and you'll have to create your own group. The first thing you have to do is offer something that attracts like-minded people. Once you make that offer, be willing to ask something of the people you are engaging with. For me, this is the most difficult part because I was raised to figure it out on my own and to be the giver. I grew up believing that to ask someone for something when you are offering something is disingenuous giving.

But the exchange actually builds bonds. Even if you are building a following, asking for something builds interaction and lets your followers know you need them. And being needed is something people crave.

If you do not trust people, they will not join you. This was also hard for me to accept. I've had a difficult time relinquishing complete control, and the people I work with can feel it. They don't feel needed or trusted and consequently become disengaged from me. People end up appreciating my work from afar instead of joining me in my work.

Only a few people can get themselves in a situation where they are successful despite being aloof from their group or set of followers. This usually happens when something they produce connects with a larger audience by hooking into a popular sentiment. The viral phenomenon can be an engine for this. However, this model is not necessarily sustainable. At some point, your people want validation from you. I always look to J. D. Salinger as an example of this. His novel *The Catcher in the Rye* is a classic that caught fire with readers across generations. But after it became popular, Salinger locked himself away. Fortunately, he made a living off that one book. But how many of us can produce *The Catcher in the Rye*?

The other way to succeed while being aloof is to have a partner who makes connections for you. For example, once actors have been said to have "made it," they have publicists who create opportunities for engagement with fans. But this sometimes results in awkward circumstances. How many strained interview setups have we seen where reluctant actors are put on the hot seat?

In any situation, being aloof is a huge risk. Your audience is fickle and will move on if they aren't getting what they need and don't feel valued. Build a group. There is power in numbers.

THE POWER OF TEACHING

I'm smart. Why should I listen to people? Why can't I just figure it out on my own?

This is related to the previous concept of the power of a group (and networking). Why? Because when you listen to the insights of someone who's put in the time and effort and learn from their experience, you can leapfrog past their stopping point to continue the work that interests you and move toward success. Think about where aviation would be if everyone had to build an experimental aircraft in their bicycle shop. We build on the learning of others—this is what makes learning from others so powerful.

In my undergraduate program, I was given the freedom to experiment. But I wasn't given much guidance because no one at my university taught sound design (my passion). My lighting-design professor taught me a lot, but I was hungry for so much more.

After graduation, I wanted to go to graduate school because I knew I could learn from others who had been doing the work longer and had more experience than I did. Graduate school made my brain hurt (in a good way) because instead of intimately learning a little bit of information each day through doing something, my brain was taking in large amounts of information passed down from others every hour (and on top of that, we had experiential learning). Graduate school was injecting me with a super serum. (I would later learn that this serum was not preparing me to meet the challenges of capitalism—

but that was why I moved to Los Angeles to learn business from successful people—and why I am writing this book.)

Knowledge is like a baton. The teacher passes it to you, and once you've gained your own knowledge and expertise, you pass it on to someone else. When focusing on how to pass your knowledge on, you naturally whittle down what you actually know. You get to challenge the information you have gathered and figure out what is worth sharing, why it's important, and how to present it. Only when you teach something do you come to realize what you actually know, which becomes a huge boost to your confidence as you move out into the world.

Recognizing the power of teaching will help you in school and in your business-informed strategies as you decide what to do in life.

FIND YOUR STRENGTH

Ask yourself what you are good at and why. Highlight your strengths and improve your weaknesses. Take the experience you have and listen to yourself. Part of your strategic approach to education will be matching institutions with your strengths (and how well they might turn your weaknesses into strengths). To help you get a feel for how institutions and the students they attract differ, I share a few experiences from my teaching past at three different universities with three very different student populations.

BFA and the Conservatory Crowd
My first job teaching was for a bachelor of fine arts (BFA) program. These students wanted to be dancers and choreographers. They took courses other than dance because that was the game the university told them they needed to play to work with the dance instructors who would make them stronger dancers and choreographers.

These students were auditioning to be in a conservatory-type program; the conservatory being their singular focus. Everything I taught them was packaged to make their dance work more thoughtful and valuable to the conservatory. I felt like I was teaching at a mini version of the master of fine arts (MFA) program from which I had just graduated.

BA and the Academically Inclined Student

When I moved to a bachelor of arts (BA) program at a graduate research institute, the students felt more academic. These were students who were used to getting good grades. These were students who were good at taking tests. They were good at following directions, and they wanted to know the answers. They were, however, resistant to thinking for themselves. Their viewpoint of life was that life was school and that the self-directed stuff was extra. In hindsight, I realized this was because they had only ever lived in school.

Many of these students didn't know what they'd do once they graduated. One told me she came to the university because she'd been offered a full-ride scholarship. Another told me they came to because it was the only university in the system that had accepted them—and their parents said they had to go to a school in the University of California system. They only started exploring options once they got to the university. No one I talked to had a plan for after graduation.

The department where I taught was also unique in that we had production requirements—at least we tried to have them. The UC system was set up as a graduate research institute, not as a conservatory. This meant that all of its courses were supposed to promote scholarship and not practical application. I worked in theatre, where the scholarship was realized in its practical application. And in order to sell this to the administration, we had strict guidelines on what a student was actually allowed to do. They were at school to learn how to think critically, not to develop a skill.

As a result, we had the most hands-off theatre department I ever experienced. A student could be a theatre major and never get good at anything theatre. Only a few dedicated students were allowed to do things.

State University and the Academically Disadvantaged

When I moved to a state university in an economically depressed area, the student population changed again. Many of the students came from impoverished areas. They were the first in their families to go to college, and most were not scholars. They had poor writing and communication skills. One person told me that the theatre department accepted the students who couldn't cut it in other departments. We were the last stop before trade school or no school. I refused to accept that we had "the remedial students," but, in general, the students in my classes loved to give me reasons for why they couldn't do the work.

Nevertheless, their willingness to try their hand at creating productions was refreshing. Many students came from blue-collar backgrounds and knew how to work on projects. And since the California State University system was not a graduate research institute, the department could actually officially support their endeavors.

This was not, however, a conservatory. These students were not hand-picked for their drive and talent, and many had life complications that stopped them from becoming productive students. School was an afterthought. Their poverty, social life, families, and jobs came first. My CSU students threw life barriers in front of their learning like I had never seen before. In general, these students were well-meaning messes.

What Kind of Student Am I?

Working with these varied populations got me thinking about what kind of student I was.

I was good at learning but also liked to create music, and I liked welding, as taught by my shop friends. I liked learning but was constantly running from possible rejection, so I never applied for any accolades. I did not go to a conservatory, and I did not apply for scholarships. I did not even try to get into any organizations. I buckled down and worked hard. I let my work speak for me because I was afraid to speak for myself. As a result, I got stuck—over and over again.

It's a good idea to honestly assess what kind of student you are, to zero in on your strengths and be keenly aware of your weaknesses.

Driven to Succeed, but in What? Try to Fully Understand Your Options

Why do schools want you? Why do you want to attend particular schools? Specifically, what will you get from a school given the student you are? Think of your education as a business plan. Research all variables and projections. Your plan may not be foolproof, but you will be in a better situation as your needs change.

DEFINING YOUR BRAND

Once you define your strengths, hone the way you describe yourself. People are more complex than a simple tagline, yet, to simplify our lives, we stereotype or "brand" those around us. "That girl is an athlete." "That guy is a bookworm." "That woman is a numbers-cruncher." Because of this, I have found it's important to brand yourself before others do it for you.

For example, during some background acting work, Hollywood branded me as a dad. I was not a dad and saw myself as the cool "loner" guy who rode a motorcycle. But my look didn't fit that stereotype for others. In order to be a biker (according to them), I'd need facial hair, tattoos, muscles, and scars. I had to accept that my baseline look was that of a dad.

As far as what I do, I am a filmmaker/producer, writer, public speaker, and video coach. That's a lot of things, and that can confuse people. After some thought, I found that when I focused on the subject matter that intrigued me (wealth, capitalism, education, and societies) instead of the products I made, my brand became much more clear. My goal in life is to grow people into wealth and to create the things that support that directive.

Simplifying with Stereotypes

Think about who you are both personally and publicly. Think about what you do both privately and publicly. Finally, think about how you want to present yourself to the public. Try to think about the future.

What is the concise story you can share that is accurate now and that you think will be accurate in the future?

This is probably going to be difficult. At forty, it took me eight months of intense thinking about what parts of me I wanted to present and how I wanted to present them. At forty-five, I still regularly attend networking events to test ideas and pitch to people to get their reactions.
But being able to brand yourself in a way that conveys the value you can bring to a group, be it a university or employer, will serve you well at every stage of life.

PART TWO—THE BUSINESS PART

BUSINESS IS NOT THE DEVIL

"Money is bad." "Making money is the antithesis of legitimacy." "Do things for the passion, and success will follow." I have heard these things my entire life.

This is what we teach each other.

To the public, making money is not the cool thing. It's put in the same category as winning the lottery. It's great to have money, but making money is a gross and self-serving thing. We don't even like to freely talk about money. It's treated as a dirty little secret. I think this may come from the perception that the rich are heartless puppet masters.

Because of this, it is difficult to market building wealth. It's easier to motivate people to follow their passion with images of firefighting, photographing vistas, or even mixing things into beakers. Building a scalable business is a difficult image to capture and make exciting to the viewer. Meetings, phone calls, spreadsheets, and emails do not generally thrill or inspire. It doesn't photograph as well as charging into a burning building.

Even though wealth-building is hard to market (other than to show an abundance of wealth through pictures of yachts, cash, and exotic locations), it's a needed skill. A business friend of mine always said, "Just because you can run a restaurant doesn't mean you can own a restaurant." Knowing how to exploit an opportunity to make money does not necessarily have anything to do with making sure there is food available for customers.

I think businesspeople are also generally okay with not marketing what they do because the people who can run the business end of a restaurant do better if others don't know how to do it. Business owners cut down on the competition, and the business does best if there are more people willing to buy a meal rather than create a restaurant. Business owners flourish when customers trade the stability of a consistent paycheck for the knowledge of how to create perceived value in products and services.

The owners gain a veritable monopoly on earning potential this way. And what customers often refuse to admit is that they actually control the future of a business, but it takes discipline, which customers have no desire to exhibit. The owners know that their customers will always respond to the ease of buying and the mania of the purchase. So they work to make their products irresistible and easy to buy.

The public complains about how much Jeff Bezos makes, but the public still buys from his store. (I cannot name his store because I want to sell this book on a competitor's platform and they want no mention of his store. But, you can look it up. I guarantee that you are familiar with it.)

THE MYTH OF THE SLEAZY SALESMAN

Why do "sales" have such a bad reputation?

As I was growing up, my parents always talked about the sleazy car salesman. In movies, there was often a sleazy car salesman trying to manipulate the protagonist in one way or another. I grew up with this image in my brain and a strong aversion to sales. I saw it as one of the lowest forms of making a living.

And I carried this judgment with me into adulthood. Somehow buying things was seen as good, but selling things seemed corrupt. When I moved out of the world of the professional consumer and into the world of commerce, I realized that in this world of capitalism, everything is a product, and everyone is ultimately selling something. Salespeople just happen to be better at it.

Because of this, I'd like to take apart the myths or, rather, stereotypes, surrounding sales.

Salespeople Will Sell You Junk
The job of the salesperson is to sell you joy. They will always work to make you feel good about your purchase. It is your job to research what you are buying.

Salespeople Will Not Give You a Fair Price
The job of the salesperson is to reap the highest profit margin possible. He or she needs to buy stuff too. It is your job to do the

research that gives you an understanding of what a fair price might be in any negotiation.

Salespeople Are Nice to You Only to Get a Sale
Salespeople are people too. They like having friendly interactions. That's why they are in sales. Yes, they want to make a sale, but they are probably being nice to you because they like being nice to you.

Salespeople Are Manipulative
Absolutely—but not in an insidious way. Their job is to get you excited about what you're buying. You also want to be excited about what you're buying. If you aren't excited, you won't buy it. They will figure out your need and offer you something that fulfills that need. Think of them as a legal form of happy drugs. Their goal is to solve your problems with products or services.

Salespeople Are Phonies
Some are. It is your job to do your due diligence. As you launch your own products or services, you will realize that one must always walk this line between being attractive to your customer and being grounded in reality, with enough proof of your work to gain your customer's confidence.

THE BUSINESS MINDSET

How Do You View the World?

Thinking like a business person is different than thinking like an employee. Here are some ideas to help you in devising a plan to sell what you do.

Find a Problem to Solve

In order to make money, you need to find a problem you can solve for consumers. If you create art, what solution does that art provide and for who? For example, I met a portrait artist who specializes in creating family portraits that cannot be photographed because someone in the family has died.

Be Attractive

Be as attractive as you can, but at the same time, prove you are real. People are attracted to attractive people. This attractiveness can be physical, mental, or emotional. By far, the strongest attraction is emotional (as all purchasing is based on emotion), but the other two don't hurt. Work on all three and be the most attractive person you can be. At the same time, work on your business foundation and proofs of concept, because potential clients will constantly run little tests to make sure you are real. Your client has to feel good about you and has to have proof that what they are buying is legitimate.

Cynicism Is Not Allowed

As a business person, you are not allowed to be cynical. Cynicism kills business. You are building a good story for someone. You and your client/customer want it to be a good story. Any criticism of that story ruins the consumer's confidence and will cause your client/customer to walk away. If you are a cynical person, you need to learn how to put your cynicism away. If you can't, become an employee and help your boss see through other people's facades. Business owners cannot be cynical. They have to be cheerleaders and motivators. If people continue to be ignorant and cynical, they will continue to be poor. (Note: Business owners must be analytically critical, but critical analysis is not the same as cynicism. Cynicism is negative, pessimistic thought.)

Balance, Consistency, and Innovation

Know when to continue trying and when to try something else. There are two competing but coexisting schools of thought in business. One holds that doing the same thing over and over again and expecting a different result is insanity. The other holds that business comes with consistency. So if you run a workshop and no one shows up, do you run it again? If you run it and only two of forty slots get filled, do you still run it? The trick is to run the other variables in your head to see if you'll learn something new from repeating it and if you can afford the cost no matter the outcome.

Keep a Positive Outlook

You can successfully run your business on positive feelings even when you don't have positive things happen, but it's best to also address negative things constructively and realistically. Unless you have a product that is exclusive and sells itself, you cannot run your business on negative feelings. Customers and clients do not need, and will shy away from, negativity. My rule for running a business is to believe in the best but plan for the worst.

PAY YOURSELF

Your financial life is a roller coaster that has ups and downs. At some point, you will make money. Then you may spend more money than you make. After that, you might make less money but inherit some other money. Then you might lose the money or have to spend it on an emergency.

My point is that life is unpredictable. But in general, we know that as we get older, we lose the ability or inclination to continue to make money. If you can put money away throughout your life and have it grow using compound interest, you set yourself up to have money after you stop actively making it. My grandfather always told me to pay myself first, but I never knew what that meant. When I was nineteen, I bought a Harley-Davidson and went to him saying, "Look, Grandpa, I paid myself first!" He just shook his head and replied, "That's not what 'pay yourself first' means."

We have bought into the world of immediate gratification. (My Harley was a prime example of that.) People who understand how the money game works are becoming rich, while those who don't understand it are struggling. More and more people have become part of the "working poor" or just the poor. I want to help you scale back the impulse for instant gratification and learn the basics of wealth-building in order that you may try to balance some of the wealth in this country on your own.

One simple step toward that end is to follow my grandfather's advice and pay yourself first. Though it may be difficult initially, stop spending money on things that give you immediate gratification. Take what you would have spent and put it in stable growth opportunities (do your research). Starbucks may get upset at the potential downturn in sales, but they are smart, and I'm sure they will survive.

THE COST OF VALUE

How Much Are You Worth?

There are two ways to look at how much money you can make:

I am worth X to Y because . . .
or
The products I offer are worth X to Y because . . .

The first perspective is very much an employee's viewpoint. This formula puts you in relation to an employer: My boss will or should pay me X because that is comparable to other competitive salaries; I make X amount for the company, so I am worth a defined percent of that; or I provide a special value to the organization, and I need X amount to stay.

The second is a business person's viewpoint. You don't have a value. Your products have value, and they are worth however much a customer will pay for them. You know that value can change based on the amount of happiness you can bring to your customer. Your product's value is based on your customer's emotions, and you work to show the customer that you can make them happy.

The first approach is less work to reach a consistent payout. But it is also more difficult to change once the payout is set.

The second approach is arguably more work, and it doesn't necessarily have a clear path to success. But once you are successful at a payout, and once you are able to scale it, your profits can be endless.

One appealing benefit of being an employee is the promise of stability. Once you get a job and understand what your role is at that job, you can focus on other things, like having a family and mowing the lawn. As a stable cog in your employer's machine, you enjoy the promise of stability in return.

Finding the business (the opportunity to sell) is the heart of the company. It's the fuel. Without a customer to buy the company's product, the machine stops. And finding the customer can be a challenge. Sometimes it's easy because the need for the product, the position of the business, the desire of the customer, and the resources of the company all align. However, it often takes tremendous effort to put those pieces in order and to keep the company in good standing.

Because of this, business owners do not have the luxury of a consistent paycheck. Their profits can potentially be huge as long as the machine is running well. So their life is dictated by maintaining the health of the machine.

Within these two extremes are variables. Employees lose their jobs and/or make a lot of money, and owners don't take care of their business and/or have time to spend with their family. The main point is, if you build the business, you take on more control and risk. If you are an employee, you take on less control but have less risk.

In today's economy, I suggest doing a bit of both to cover your bases. I suggest working for someone *and* owning a business. Each will give you an appreciation for how business runs. I didn't really own a business until 2015, and because of that, money was just something my employer never gave me enough of. I never really tried to understand why I was only getting the money I was. This stifled and frustrated me. I knew I was missing something, but I didn't know what.

I was in the same boat as many college students hitting the job market with their shiny new degrees. I hadn't strategically mapped out and followed my education, and I certainly wasn't aware of any of the principles I'm sharing with you now. I'm hoping I can help you avoid the pitfalls and frustrations that plagued me.

So, have a job AND open an online store, or start your business AND occasionally work for your friend. Or spend your life with a goal that you will position yourself to start a lucrative business AND at the same time be an attractive employee to someone.

The employee versus employer life outlook can be very different. But the key for maximum survivability is to grow both outlooks simultaneously.

THE SLIDING VALUE OF TIME

What is your time worth?

Do people pay you for time away from your family?
Do people pay you for your time in comparison to others' time?
Do people pay for your time in regard to how much money you make for them?
Do people pay you for your time in regard to how much you spent on your education?
Do people pay you for your time in regard to how much money you will potentially make for others?

A public speaker once told me that his clients paid a minimum of $1,500 for a keynote speech because of:

- his expertise
- his time away from his family
- his time and ability onstage

They would pay more if his celebrity helped sell conference tickets.

I paid $400 an hour to an entertainment attorney I didn't like and $250 an hour to one I did. The more expensive lawyer was in Beverly Hills; the less expensive was in Hollywood. I'm sure I paid extra for the building in Beverly Hills.

As a university professor (with a terminal degree), I put in a third more hours and made a third less money than an elementary school teacher (with a teaching credential and a master's degree) in the same region of the country. I think this was because the teacher had a stronger union negotiating their contract.

Your time is always negotiable depending on the leverage you have.

But should we be thinking about time this way? Can you get away from time models? Can you focus on the worth of delivering happiness to customers?

A woman who offered an online course on how to sell products using an online store sold her course to a Chinese clientele for $888. The number eight, you see, is lucky in China, so it was important that the price had eights in it. She, however, decided the course was worth more than that because she increased the sales of her customers by an average of 30 to 50 percent. Her mentor suggested she sell the same course for $1,888. She did, and her sales did not drop.

My mind was blown. The same course increased by $1,000, and no one batted an eye. Value is truly determined by what someone is willing to buy "it" for. And if you're delivering happiness, however your client defines that happiness, the value will be high.

THE SLIDING REALITY OF MONEY

What Is Money? How Do You Get Paid—And for What?

Let's say you get your first job. You are a cashier at a snack bar (my first job). You make money by trading your time to operate the snack bar. You own nothing and are paid commensurate with the profits of the snack bar and your ability to assist in the earning of those profits. Snack bars sell relatively inexpensive items, so the goal is to sell many items throughout your shift. However, you are paid a flat rate, so you have no incentive to sell more (unless you try to justify a raise). Your boss pays you in cash at the end of each day. Your time is monetized at a set rate.

Now, let's say you are an artist and a friend suggests you feature your drawings on a T-shirt. You find a company that will print your drawing on the shirt and ship it out at $10 a shirt. You decide to sell your shirt for $20 so that every time you sell a shirt, you earn $10. Everyone at your school loves the shirt and buys one. People are told where to buy it through word of mouth—so you don't have to spend money on advertising. It goes viral. Now your time is no longer being monetized. Now your product is being monetized. You get a check sent to you by the T-shirt company at the end of each month. You don't have a bank account, so you have to sign the check over to your mom, who then gives you cash. Your mom has just exchanged bank money (a promissory note or check) for government money. You end up making more money than your mother is comfortable giving to you in cash, so she has you set up a bank account to store bank money. As long as you set up a savings account too, the bank doesn't charge you to hold your bank money there.

Next, let's say you have a friend who knows the owner of a very rich company who might want to use your drawing in a marketing campaign. Your friend introduces you to the owner, and the owner decides to use that drawing in a campaign. Your friend gets paid an introduction fee commensurate with a projection of how much profit this campaign will make the company. You are paid a licensing fee (so the company can use your artwork) that is also in line with a projection of how much the campaign will earn the company.

Now you aren't being paid for your time or product. You are being paid for the earning potential of your intellectual property (your drawing), and your friend is being paid based on the earning potential of his network (you). The company transfers your earnings from their bank account into your savings account.

In this scenario, the money you are paid did not come directly from customers. It came from potential customers. Did the company that paid you have a store of dollar bills they physically moved to your bank? They did not. They most likely paid you with a bank credit. Just like consumers buy goods with credit from banks, businesses also pay for things on credit. Banks want customers to use credit because banks then earn interest for taking the risk of fronting the money, and businesses use credit because if they take a risk, they only potentially lose credit.

Money As Energy

Money is not a hard-and-fast entity. It is a tool to use in life. My friend says that money is energy. Those who use it intelligently stabilize their ability to live. Those who do not use it intelligently waste it or get stuck in the debt/interest traps lenders and businesses set for the ignorant.

I keep myself from getting wrapped up in the beliefs that we have about money (e.g., "money is power"; "more money, more problems"; "money solves everything"; "I need money to be happy"; "credit is king"; etc.) by challenging myself to pursue the simple needs of an animal. An animal eats, sleeps, bathes, relieves itself, shelters itself, and entertains itself. Humans have turned to exchanging money for these things. I focus on the financial decisions that will fulfill my "animal" list for my entire lifetime.

FREEING MONEY FROM MORALITY

Got Morals? You Can Still Make Money.

Money is a component of a strategy. Paying money is a show of confidence in someone or something. Money is a placeholder for goods or services. Money is an exchange currency for good feelings. Money is neither moral or immoral. People can be accused of being immoral. Money cannot be.

The inclination to bleed people's morality onto a transaction is prevalent. In fact, people who work with money use this to manipulate customers. For example, nonprofits ask you to donate to their cause out of moral obligation. Also, when giving a gift to someone, the more expensive the gift, the more the giver must care about the recipient (like wedding rings). We have tied morals to money to the point of strangling ourselves.

When my mother passed away, a family member sent money to my father because she wanted to help and thought we could use it for something. My father freaked out. He did not want to gain financially from his wife's death. You could distract yourself arguing this difference in morality, or you could just simply put the morality down and work with the cash in the room. As it stood, my father told me, "Put it somewhere, but not in your wallet." He didn't want to touch it, and he didn't want me to touch it.

So the money that family member sent sits in a basket on my father's mantel—doing nothing. In order to relieve my father's stress, I set up a GoFundMe account so other people who wanted to help "could do something." I decided the donations should go to the church my family attended—because it made sense to me (my morality). I don't know if GoFundMe took a management fee. Is that moral? Does that matter? I don't know how the church will use the donated funds, but I'm guessing their morality will align with my mother's wishes.

Morality Complicates Commerce

Some people would argue that morality is important in commerce, but then we get bogged down in personal and changing moral viewpoints. One that spins my head is gaming (gambling) on riverboats. Something illegal on land is legal if done on a floating platform that travels on water running through that land. What are we doing?

I completely understand why we tie morals to our money, but to succeed in business, you have to make sure those morals do not become a hindrance. This hit me most closely during the housing crisis of 2008. I was told to always pay my debts. And I bought a house for the first time in 2006 using my great credit score. But in 2008, I was part of a cutback at work and wasn't able to make the loan payment. When I called my bank to work something out, they told me I would have to stop paying them before they would even talk to me.

Morally, this made no sense to me. But actionably, it made sense to the bank because I had to prove to them that I couldn't make the payment. My word was not enough. I later found out that part of my mortgage payment paid for an insurance policy the bank took out on me in case I didn't pay my mortgage. They didn't have faith in me after all. They simply needed to cover their investment.

Also, the bank was hoping that my morality would encourage me to pick up more work (and possibly break myself) in order to continue to pay on the original loan. They cared about the loan, not my circumstances. My job didn't care about the morality of putting me on work furloughs. They cared about clearing their budgets. The whole situation caused me to question my reality because I was the only one who seemed depressed that I couldn't make this loan work. It was affecting my ability to think strategically, and I was in denial of the reality in front of me. My morality was stifling my financial success.

So, what do we do? Default on loans? Lie? Steal? I say no. But we can't pretend plans won't potentially fall apart. And if they do, save your morality for the people around you and not for the money people are using. Spending money is a risk, but it also benefits those around you. Be aware of the risks and try to mitigate them, but still push forward with your opportunities.

FINDING OPPORTUNITIES

Always Try to Keep an Open Mind

People say, "follow your passion" because many people get into a situation of simply doing things for money and find their lives to be hollow. However, I have experienced the other side of that—where I have only ever followed my passions with no deference for making money and because my passions are not shared by others, I don't make any money at them.

Because of this, I say you always have to find the opportunities in your passion. Even people who say they don't care about money do not want to struggle to live. If you follow your passions simply for the sake of following your passions, you will struggle.

What do I mean by looking for the opportunities in your passion? The following is an example of a strategy I tried to implement in my life. It shows the reasoning behind my professional choices.

As I've said, I come from a theatre background. (You can tell because I spell "theatre" the English way). Theatre is poor. This is because the profit margins in theatre are slim and the overhead is high. The worst part is, it's not very scalable. It's not like a movie where once it's made (even though it cost a lot of money to make), you have the potential to sell it in perpetuity. With theatre, your main opportunity to make money is at the performance. Because of this, the less it costs to produce, the bigger the audience you can get, and the more opportunities you can create for merchandising, the better off you are.

Theatre also has a perception problem in the United States. It is seen as elitist. Part of this is because of the high ticket prices producers have to charge in order to keep afloat, but the other reason is because it is seen as providing more substance than entertainment. The story, the art, and the social relevance are marketed rather than the fun, the intrigue, or the excitement a movie would use for its marketing. It is marketed as smart and artsy entertainment, like an art-house film would be. And the market for an art-house film is small. If you cast unknown actors in the show, the market grows even smaller. Musicals and Shakespeare plays are the only theatre productions that seem to appeal to a broader market because musicals promise fun escapism, and Shakespeare plays promote a familiar brand.

So I turned to other live entertainment to make money. Concerts have lower overhead and can be produced in spaces with more seats and under the brand of the named talent. Conventions became another option because people are willing to pay corporate rates for tickets, and much of the time the corporations look at the convention as a marketing expense (instead of their money-making engine). This was my strategy in looking for opportunity while using my passion.

Theatre is also seen as a valuable storytelling craft by some in other industries with more money. So if you can be recognized as a theatre authority to someone with money who cares about the "legitimacy" of theatre as an art form, you could position yourself for lucrative opportunities.

None of this worked for me. I started working for a production company that supported concerts and conventions, but they just needed me to work in their shop. As I worked my way up and was just starting to work on-site (for more money), the company was bought out by a larger company. I ended up moving into academia (which is another poor industry) because I had the opportunity. Once in academia, I was distracted by life and stopped seeking outside opportunities. I also never found someone with money who valued my theatre background.

That said, I still believe that continually finding the opportunity in your passion is better than blindly starving or selling your soul for cash. But it can be hard work, and it can take a long time. The silver lining in my situation is that I have left a trail of work behind me that I am proud of and I am now building on my previous work in order to open new opportunities.

So follow your passion but also look for the opportunities that will pay you. Because if you don't have money, you can't follow your passion —unless your passion is to be poor.

BUILDING INTEREST

Why Might People Be Interested in You or What You Have?

Why do we seek out or buy things? Because things give us joy. How do we know they will give us joy before we seek them out or buy them? We've seen others experiencing joy from them. This is through word of mouth, publicity, and/or advertising. The more contact we have with something that promises to give us joy and the more we see others enjoying the product or work, the more apt we are to want to purchase it ourselves and the more excited we become about buying it.

Awards or reviews also tell others your stuff is good. We buy things from people we know, like, and trust, and a review or award can get people to trust that your product or work is worth their attention.

So for you to build interest in what you have to offer, you have to have a "thing." Your thing (at least) has to be clearly defined by you. If you don't have it, you won't be able to communicate it. Many creatives fall into this problem when they try to build interest in an idea that isn't fully fleshed out. This is evidenced in a person who has an idea for a business but never takes the time to build a business plan for it or a writer who has an idea for a story but never writes it down.

Even if you are a model and your thing is simply your being—your image—you have to decide what part of your being you want to present and how you want to present it so you can create a plan to build interest in you. This means you need a business plan in order to build a successful marketing plan. Even if your attempts at building interest are successful at catching the public's attention, without a well-defined and functioning business plan, you are in jeopardy of the interest in your thing crashing because it has no infrastructure to sustain it. A perfect example is the Fyre Festival. If you aren't familiar with it, please look it up. The Fyre Festival was brilliantly marketed and generated great ticket sales. But when festival-goers arrived at the event, there was no event. That case study is a flagship example of what a "marketing first" model can get you.

Give Your Product a Presence

This is most easily done with a website landing page. (This could be a sponsored page through a social media like Facebook). Make sure the thing—your product—is clearly defined. Confusion pushes people away.
Then come up with different ways to talk about and present your thing. Send these communications via platforms that can reach the people who would like your thing. If you are hosting an event for young mothers, choose platforms that attract or feature young mothers. Before the internet, people would visit locations frequented by young mothers and hand out fliers.
In your communication, define what benefit it is to THEM and invite them to a dialogue. Give them a reason to visit your web page. You are trying to build familiarity, and if you can get them to not only see your advertisement but also visit your page, you have scored two contacts for the price of one.

You also want to be able to directly contact the people who show interest so you can keep them apprised of other things they might be interested in. A tendency is to collect emails to then blast out to your subscriber lists. Automation is overused nowadays, and I am seeing a backlash in it. Keep direct communications as personal as possible, as well as strategic. You want people to know, like, and trust you—and not know, hate, and be annoyed by you.

Build Excitement with a Story

Build a story arc in your communications. Build intrigue. Build exclusivity. Build a time limit. Have fun with your communications. People like to be taken on a journey, so take them on a journey with your ads and promise a better journey when they attend your event (or buy your product).

Seek opportunities for continued engagement. Add raffle opportunities, or games and quizzes. Think of your audience as those you would engage with personally, and they will start to respond in kind. This may sound like a lot of work, but if you are not someone they have already put up on a pedestal, you will not get the one-sided worship current celebrities or social icons *seem* to get without having to work for it.

By the way, those celebrities and social icons have worked for their positions. You just didn't see the work. Most people who "come on the scene from seemingly nowhere" have been working in obscurity for a while. Building interest takes time.

Always be sure to deliver on your thing and follow up with people after the thing. Build, build, build. People will start to be interested in what you are building. At every opportunity, prove your reality. Do not be a Fyre Festival.

Finally, never stop building interest—even when people don't seem interested. Maybe pivot your thing. Maybe change your message. But don't stop. Your visibility builds on itself. Then, if you have to disappear for a while, interested people will ask, "Where have you been?" Your reappearance could even build interest.

UNDERSTANDING MOTIVATIONS

Why Do We Buy Things?

People know what they want but not necessarily what they need. It is your job to get them what they want and make sure you deliver beyond their expectations. The last thing you want is a remorseful buyer. People want to feel good when buying your product and to continue feeling good after buying your product. In order to illustrate these concepts, I share my experience with a company I hired to promote the launch of a book I released.

The company promised that my book would be a best seller on a certain large retail website. They absolutely delivered on this promise. What they did not make completely clear (before I paid them) was that the term "best seller" was not tied to purchasing my book. The retailer defines a sale as any download—even free downloads. So this company placed my book on strategic retail bookshelves and promoted its free download to strategic websites. In a weeklong campaign, my book was downloaded enough times from enough of the right bookshelves to qualify as a "Best Seller." I didn't "sell" (exchange money for goods) anything, and I made no money.

The promotion company suggested I generate revenue by using the book as an advertisement in order to secure paid speaking engagements and leads to customers who would buy my coaching products. They actually taught a business model that used the "best-seller" title as the start of the sales process. It is a valid model, but they didn't lead with that information because authors *want* their book to be a "best seller," and it's easy to lead with that phrase. In the author's understanding, the sale would be the end of the transaction. In reality, the "sale" of the book is the entry into a larger sales funnel.

I would argue that the choice to lead with the promise of best-seller status is a bit misleading. It would be more forthright to lead with the "Free + Shipping" business model, but very few customers would buy into a program called "give your book away for free and upsell them on other products." Customers don't want to buy work. They want to buy solutions. The company sold people what they wanted and then taught them what they needed. This opens you up for buyer's remorse and bad reviews. Even though they delivered on their promise, I won't recommend the company. I felt they withheld information in their sales process.

Know that potential customers want to purchase a product that will help them and the only reason they want to know about you is to make sure they can know, like, and trust both you and what you are selling. If your brand is trustworthy enough (through familiarity), customers may buy anything from your brand. People buy anything Apple because Apple has done the work of building familiarity, exclusivity, stability, and innovation. You are trying to do the same.

Endorsements by well-known and trusted individuals, competition wins, and even titles (like "best seller") can bring confidence to potential customers. Word of mouth (endorsement by a potential customer's friend) is also powerful. The trust in that friend is transferred to you, and if their friend says, "Buy this; it's the greatest," they are likely to buy it.

Also know that a customer stays with you when they are allowed to purchase on their own time line. If you pressure people to buy, you may risk their regret or even turn them away. This is a tricky time line to manage because, as the seller, you need to make sales in order to survive. The goal is to knock down any barriers the customer may have to buying and show them how they need your product or service in their lives. Show them you have the solution to their problem rather than pressuring them into buying something.

Understanding what people want and knowing how to present it to them can sometimes seem manipulative. Try not to live in that headspace. Connect with people. Find out what they *need*. If you can provide the solution to their problem, show them. Many salespeople say they "save lives" or "help people." That is the right headspace to live in; just don't say it out loud. Leave those catchphrases to the paramedics and nurses. Let them have something. They probably won't make as much money as you will.

YOU HAVE TO SELL

You Have to Do It

Many people are averse to sales. They view it as a manipulative and annoying trade. Yet we love to buy things. How can we view one side of an interaction as fun but the other side as abhorrent? I think it comes from the perception that someone with money to spend is powerful, while someone with something to sell is needy.

In fact, the best salespeople put their product or service in a position of desire, where clients or customers come to them. The television show *Futurama* showed this best when the character Fry told a vendor to shut up and take his money. My business coach often said that when we sell something, we view ourselves as the actor onstage hoping to be cast, but we instead need to be the casting director looking to cast clients.

A friend of mine talked about not minding the sale structure but wanting to approach the salesperson instead of having the salesperson reach out to them. This is called inbound marketing—where a company or product spends time and money building something attractive that draws customers to them. Much of the time, this is expensive and slow, and in order to do it and stay in business, the company either needs to have saved a lot of money (or credit) or do outbound marketing and direct sales to bring money in.

Selling something *is* playing on a buyer's psychology. But as long as the buyer is looking for that feeling the seller wants to give them, and as long as the seller delivers on what they promise, there is nothing wrong with that transaction. After all, when we buy something, we are buying good feelings and a solution to our problems. And you, as the seller, are the person providing those things.

BEING SCALABLE

How Can You Be Bigger Than You?

Owning a business can be your job, and you can be successful in owning and operating that business. But if you keep that business running on the back of your personal labor, that business stops when you stop. Your earning potential is also limited to the work you can personally get done. In order to grow the business, your offering needs to be scalable.

Ask yourself this question: Can I grow what I love to do into something that can be sold multiple times to multiple people with a reduction of my direct effort? This is the goal of scalability.

If you play guitar and write original music, can you record that music and license its use for YouTube videos? If you teach guitar, instead of teaching one on one, can you make video tutorials and sell those videos as an online course? If you have a special cleaning service for cars, can you hire and train others to clean like you do so you can clean more cars? All of these are examples of scaling your work. The goal in business is to make present money from past work. This is what's called a passive income, and this passive income often allows a business to scale itself.

This model can even become more complex. I'll illustrate using the model touted by the "best-seller" promotion company I hired.

If you write a book, selling it to multiple people can be seen as a scale. But if your book sells for $20 a copy, every customer is only worth $20 to you. What if you could have multiple offerings for each customer who was interested in your work? First, you offer them a book for $20, but at the same time, you offer them a workbook-and-book package for $30. Then you offer them an online course for $90. After that, you offer your accelerated seminar and/or speaking services for hundreds or thousands of dollars. Instead of focusing on a single transaction, you work on building a relationship with that customer so you have multiple opportunities to keep them as a customer. Star Wars and the merchandising of the characters and stories beyond the films is a prime example of this. They spent the time to find the customer who likes their products and have found ways to continue returning to that customer.

There are many different ways to scale your business, but a mentor of mine said the best approach is to find a way that frees you from trading your time for money.

AUTOMATION

How Can You Be Bigger Than You but Still Be Human?

There are many tools out there that can act as force multipliers for your business. If you are running a company, how wise is it to spend your time individually sending out emails to potential customers? How beneficial is it to spend time editing your video content instead of creating sales opportunities? Arguably, you can find someone to write your videos or edit your content. And until you can afford that, artificial intelligence is now at a point where a robot can do these services for you.
Just be careful. Robot work still needs to be cleared by a human before it's sent out. As good as robots are, when they try to be human, they don't sound quite right. Some customers don't mind, but I would argue that your personal touch can make you stand out in this automated world. You absolutely need to balance your time and focus on the things only you can do. But always weigh the cost of your time versus the cost of your integrity.

I once hired someone who forgot to remove me from his autodrip contact campaign after I had hired him. I spoke with him twice a week, yet occasionally I would receive texts from him saying, "Glen, I just wanted to check in to see how your business is going. I care about your success." I would text back, "We talked yesterday. You know how it's going. Please take me off of your automation."

I knew this man was very good at what he did, and I knew he knew his stuff, but those texts put him in jeopardy of looking foolish to his clients. For this reason, I suggest you play with robots carefully.

FOCUS VERSUS DIVERSIFICATION

Some say do one thing well. Others say to diversify in order to spread your risk.

Some say the definition of insanity is to do the same thing over and over but to expect a different result. Still others say that you first need to build consistency and that you can't expect an immediate result.

It's a fine balance. The trick is to find that balance for yourself. The best way to do this is to take the lessons and criticisms of others to heart but also constantly listen to yourself. If something doesn't seem right, try to find out why.

Here's an example:

A publicity professional told me that the best way to get exposure was to write a book that was a follow-up to something I was already known for. I was known for a documentary on homelessness, so I wrote a companion piece to that movie. A publishing company told me the best way to earn money from my book was to use the book to secure speaking engagements. Both the publicity professional and the publishing company had a vested interest in my success since I would be hiring them for their services. They were smart to have me pay them up front because there were no guarantees to the success of that business model.

Even though the book was well reviewed, I was unable to secure consistent opportunities for publicity. And I could find no one who wanted to pay me to speak for my work or experiences with the homeless. The problem was the subject matter. No one expects homelessness to be worth money, so no one wants to pay for products surrounding homelessness. Those who read my book and saw my movie appreciated the content, but they didn't want to pay for it.

So I modified my original plan; I diversified my thing. All my homeless work has become a proof of concept for my video-coaching business. "I know video so well, I even make the homeless look good." My homeless work is important to me, and it brings me recognition— which helps me secure video-coaching clients. As it has become part of my marketing campaign for something else (though not book sales, publicity, or speaking engagements), the work is not a loss.

Singular focus can be powerful, but it can lead you down a path that (if not successful) is hard to maintain. Diversification gives you options, but you might never get anything done.

What I try to do is keep all facets of my diversification somehow feeding into the same goal. This takes work, but it is doable. It gives you a unifying story that clearly represents all your work so that no matter who you meet, your story is the same and just has layers you can share with different audiences. This unified story also helps me to be "real" in the eyes of those I'm approaching.

THE TIME IT TAKES TO BUILD A BUSINESS

Let me outline how I created a business so you can see how *not* to do it.

When I first started making entertainment in 2010, I wasn't worried about how to make money. My accountant told me it was a hobby and not a business. I also bought items for my hobby, which I used at my regular job. My accountant told me my employers should be providing any job-related equipment and that I should not be buying equipment for my business and then using it at my job. I also didn't have a clear definition of my business.

Come 2015, I still did not have a true understanding of my business. I could not let go of my past identity even though I wanted to move in a new direction. Because I had been a designer and educator, I still put that on my card—even though I was no longer doing that work. This confused people I met. I learned I had to choose an identity, so I focused on filmmaking and producing, but I was putting myself in front of people who weren't in the filmmaking world. The confusion continued.

Finally, in 2018, I started to clearly define my identity. My business coach thought my message was still too muddy, but I worked hard to bring everything together in a cohesive story. I am a filmmaker/

producer and video coach. I make stuff and teach people how to make stuff. My business card says:

Filmmaker, Producer, Writer
Public Speaker
Video Coach

Why do I put "writer"? Because I write about what I do. Why do I put "public speaker"? Because I speak about what I do. My website says it best—"I make stuff. I teach people how to make stuff."

So, in 2018, I really started defining and setting up my business. I thought I would get "conversion" (sales) within four months. That did not happen. I was distracted with writing a book to follow my homeless documentary and with using my time as a university professor to pitch to students on helping them develop business skills before they graduated. Those endeavors built credibility, but they made me no money. I started focusing on the video-coaching component of my business and finally gained some traction.

I was still not making money, but my business systems were set up to a point I could take on other work and build my business after-hours.

So how long does it take to build a business? Sometimes you are in the right place at the right time with the right product for the right clientele and you have the right infrastructure to support it. Sometimes you are quickly positioned to feed a starving crowd. But sometimes you don't know what you are doing and it takes eight years to figure it out. And then it takes you more than a year to make a sale.

The time it takes really depends on the size of your business as well. The more moving parts you have, the longer it takes to set everything up. If you are building it yourself, that can also take longer. Having partners can help things move forward more quickly. Just make sure they are the right partners, otherwise your business can fall apart.

All of this said, you CAN do it! And it's worth it. I remember where I was when I was stuck in jobs that weren't paying me the money I needed and I had no idea how to earn more. It's been a long journey, but I am here, and if I—a theatre guy who was taught that poverty equaled legitimacy—can do it, anyone can.

ENTREPRENEURIAL CONFIDENCE

How Confident in Yourself Are You?

When I started my business, I was hesitant to claim I could deliver results if I did not have a specific proof of concept. I realized that if I expected people to trust me, I had to first trust myself.

I am not saying to " fake it till you make it." In fact, there is no faking it. You perform and work to not fail. Because just like in doing a backflip or some other physical feat, if you do not visualize your success, you will fail. You have to see all of the steps to completion and then embody that completion. If you make a misstep, you work through it to recover.

People who are good at business have confidence in their ability to work through and find solutions. Because they are not hesitant to put in the work, they also know they are the best person to do what they offer. People gravitate to others who have the solutions, and a business owner knows they will find a solution. In some way, the customer's confidence in you becomes a self-fulfilling prophecy.

This confidence in one's self can make some people pompous. Though you must have self-confidence in order to succeed, hopefully you can temper that confidence with humility and knowing that your clients or customers are just as important to your success as you are.

I don't know if this can be taught, but from my experience, it can definitely be developed and brought out in a person. For example, you can build confidence by networking with successful businesspeople.

Business networking has given me a great understanding of how to make businesses work. When I first arrived in Los Angeles, I would attend events and ask, "How do you make money?" over and over again. Understand that businesspeople put a monetary value on their information but are usually open to sharing the basics and will guide you to other resources that could be valuable to you.

Know that businesspeople also surround themselves with other businesspeople. Entrepreneurship is a wild ride, and only other entrepreneurs can keep you focused on your goal when things get crazy. The employee types will just tell you to quit and go work for someone. Other entrepreneurs you network with, however, can educate and energize you in your business endeavors.

FINDING THE THING YOU ENJOY DOING FOR PEOPLE

To succeed in business, you must find the thing you enjoy about helping people and focus on that. If your motivation is to make money, your customer will turn away from you. If your motivation is to make someone's life better, your customer will come to you.

Building a business can be hard, and there are many moving parts that can frustrate the entrepreneur. You, however, cannot live in that frustration. You have to live in a headspace of joy and service.

Obviously, you need to make money and you need to respect yourself and hold fast that you need to be compensated for your talents. But what you offer your customer/client is something that will change their life for the better—even if it is simply the momentary enjoyment of the cupcake you make. This will draw customers to you. Your joy will be attractive. A friend of mine says that the perfect balance between work and play is called charisma. Be charismatic.

What do you do if you are not charismatic? Find a partner who is. And even if you can't be charismatic, you need to find a way to be positive. Even if your product or service sells itself, you will bury yourself in despair if you can't find joy in how you help people.

Much of this sounded too "new-agey" to me when I first started down the path of entrepreneurship. But as I got into building a business, my frustrations started affecting my external relationships—which affected my business. Whether you believe in "woohoo" pep-rally stuff or not, people will pick up on your energy and respond to it. They are attracted to honest enjoyment and stay away from things that don't give them joy. Give your customers fun and joy.

REINVENTING THE WHEEL

Don't Do This If You Don't Have To

Stand on the shoulders of giants. It is easier to build your specific business by modeling an existing business. I have the awful habit of being an independent thinker. Disruptive models excite me. For example, I want people to be inspired by the homeless! And that is HARD!

When I first saw folks setting up their own online stores to market and upsell other online products to be fulfilled by other people's online stores, it seemed lazy and a bit deceitful. Yet they made money. I did not. When I saw my friends sell life insurance to Baby Boomers who were afraid they might die, I thought that was a bit sinister. They made money. I did not.

People *want* to be given a good story and a solution to their problems/fears. Baby Boomers want life insurance, but no one REALLY wants to care about homeless people. Please, change the world and make it a better place, but don't kill yourself while doing it.

The last thing I have to share is something that took me forty-five years to learn:

People who work with money, pay money. Find the money. Everything else in business comes after that. Your product or service can be amazing, but if people aren't looking to spend money on it, they won't.

CONCLUSION

Does This Make Sense?

This book is a start to the retraining of the student brain. You have been taught things in school that can be used as tools, but you have not been shown how to use those tools in order to succeed in present-day society.

At one time, there was a value put on people who were good employees. Now societies move so fast you may be needed as an employee one moment and in a position to forward your own value in another.

People have also started exploiting others for short-term gains. Making a long-term investment in a person started to go out of fashion in the 1970s and has slowly crept out of much of our work world. This may have even happened with your college education. For years we have been selling students and families on going to college while at the same time increasing the price of tuition for a degree that no longer guarantees you'll make enough money to pay your student loans back.

We tell one another to follow our passions. But we don't tell one another how to make those passions sustainable. This book is a start at giving you those tools. Know that it is just a start. These ideas should sit in the back of your head as a starting point should you decide to take your professional life into your own hands.

Again, get any education you want, but think about how you can actually use that education to help you succeed throughout life. Some people won't care or won't want to care. They will look at their education as separate from their success. That's fine. This book is just trying to keep you from getting a degree in homelessness—because unintentional poverty is not fun. Trust me.

Now, go fight to define your value!

Thanks for reading! If you enjoyed this book please write it a review at your favorite retailer. Also, remember to reach out to me with any thoughts or questions you may have at glendunzweiler.com.

www.ingramcontent.com/pod-product-compliance
Lightning Source LLC
Chambersburg PA
CBHW070436220526
45466CB00004B/1701